KINDRED SPIRITS:
HORSE RACING NAME POEMS

Kindred Spirits:
Horse Racing Name Poems

A collection of poems

by

JOSEPH A PASQUALE

BOOKS

Adelaide Books
New York / Lisbon
2020

KINDRED SPIRITS: HORSE RACING NAME POEMS
A collection of poems
by Joseph A Pasquale

Copyright © by Joseph A Pasquale
Cover design © 2020 Adelaide Books

Published by Adelaide Books, New York / Lisbon
adelaidebooks.org
Editor-in-Chief
Stevan V. Nikolic

For any information, please address Adelaide Books
at info@adelaidebooks.org
or write to:
Adelaide Books
244 Fifth Ave. Suite D27
New York, NY, 10001

ISBN: 978-1-952570-91-9

Printed in the United States of America

Contents

Foreword

This poetry collection, "Kindred Spirits: Horse Racing Name Poems" was inspired by horse racing names at current tracks across America.

It just so happened that I couldn't help but see meaning in every name attached to those lovely animals. Soon after, word associations fell into place and this experimental book was born - a poetry collection constructed exclusively of horse name combinations.

The following is a list of the race tracks where I sourced most of the actual horse names.

Woodbine	Del Mar	Churchill Downs
Zia Park	Harrah's Philadelphia	Delta Downs
Finger Lakes	Parx Racing	Gulfstream Park West
Mountaineer Park	Laurel Park	Charles Town
Golden Gate Fields	Tampa Bay Downs	Remington Park
Turfway Park	Penn National	Oaklawn Park
Turf Paradise	Woodbine Thoroughbreds	Zia Park
Northfield Park	Santa Anita	Aqueduct
Hawthorne		

In total, each horse name originated from about twenty-five race tracks across the United States. Throughout the process I worked with a poetic postulation to the following questions:

What meaning can we associate to every word we encounter?

How can we choose to interpret that meaning and then associate it again to an even greater meaning we choose to construct?

This collection was such an experiment in poetry. As tempting as it was to add or delete words, I refrained in order to maintain the material's integrity.

The book is separated into three sections to arc the reader's journey through wisdom, nature and hope.

In the appendix section you will find the actual horse racing names used to compile each expression in this book.

One of many resources one can use to verify the horse names is: Equibase.com. I hope you find your own meanings from what I found in mine. Enjoy!

KINDRED INSIGHTS

Life happens
Between

-

Buoy
Lost in the fog

Tampered character
　　　Contemplate
Owl's run

Master of excuses
Watch your words
　　　Tricky escape

Bored stiff?
Contemplate
Ideal shadow

Bored stiff
    Another secret
Nobody else

Mind reader
    Retrospection
Spiritual warfare

Boxing gloves
      Fool me once
First punch

Wise
      Under pressure,
Idiot

Idiot
      Justify
Wise

Eye of the wind
    Don't overlook
Tears of the sun

Burning shore
    I've seen the future
Add water

Eye of the river
Eye of the wind
    Blind ambition

True concern
    Decision reversed
No fear

Fire on fire
    Add water
Zero out

Easy river
      Decision reversed
Troublesome waters

No excuses
      Watch your words
Art of confusion

Valid pursuit
New heaven

Valid objection
World of trouble

Favorable outcome
Always a suspect

Yummy bear
　　Potential danger
Venomous state

The last cup
　　Tiki bar logic
Midnight rumble

Skip the talk
　　Another chance –
Kisses for love

Baby touch
      Potential danger
Mean bone

Mouse trap
      Quality interest
Expect kitten

Zimbabwe
      Passing reminder
King dollar

True wisdom,
    Potential danger:
Not for truth

Winning element
    Easy attitude

                                        Infinite wisdom
                                        -Blame angel,
                                        Not for truth

Off duty conscience
Fashionably late
Chosen facts hide the evil

Master of excuses
Next success
Famous fact

Chosen facts hide the evil
Stun nothing,
but a smile

Web cam
    Valid objection
Clean mind

Infinite wisdom
    Potential danger
Riding alone

Last kiss—
Don't overlook
First of its kind

Path dependent -
    Bridge builder
    Bridge jumper

Bridge builder
    Surprise cameo
Bridge jumper

Bridge jumper
Better way
Moral high ground

Analyze
What gives moral high ground
Understanding

True concern
      Decision reversed
There's no doubt

Faith prevails
Making sure

The day you have made
Will make way wise

KINDRED SPIRITS

Space shuttle
Orbit
Heaven's creation

Tears of the sun
Entrusted
Forest dew

Cheers to you
Cat 'n Bird
Hoppity

Joseph A Pasquale

Under the rain
    Mr. bully frog
Grass runner

River otter
    Lakeside sunset
Graceful image

    Mystical stones
    Back scatter
    Lake surprise

    Stormy river
Backscatter trout

Space shuttle
Orbit
World oftrouble

Sad Story
On the cusp
Lasting Love

Lakeside surprise
    Mr. Bully frog
Splash hit!

                    Pacific wind
                      Storm the hill
                    Sunset catch

Forest mouse
    Grass runner
Expect kitten

Grass runner
Forest dew
On my toes

Visual effect
Tears of the sun
Raining lemons

Lakeside sunset
Look at that!
Black out

Prayer boy
      Somewhere on the beach
Girl crazy

            Chocolate ice cream
            You're wonderful

Sea foam
    What a catch
Morning breeze

Pop of color
    I cried a tear
Violet blue

Ideal shadow
    Persistent threat
Boxing gloves

Owl's run –
    Proper landing
Snowy pleasure

Forest mouse
    Grass runner
Expect kitten

Tears of the sun
    Touching rainbows
Heaven's creation

Act of madness
    Imitation
I love you honey

Still beautiful
    Just in speight of it
Last kiss

Good intent
    Born in a breeze
Lost for words

Cheese on chocolate ice cream
Golden bubbles

Golden bubbles
Jumping on clouds
Lakeside sunset

Tears of the sun
Sunset catch
Mountain on fire

Looking for a smile?
　　　Look the other way
I've got issues

　　　　　　　　　　　Pepper and salt
　　　　　　　　　　　　Cheese on
　　　　　　　　　　　Red hot salsa

Clean mind
　　　Always thinking
Moral high ground

Space shuttle orbit
Eden ridge

Pure perfection
Let me sleep on it –
Gift of a star

Laughing matters
I cried a tear
Violet blue

Moon over Montana
    The ghost b dancing
Forest waltz grace

Dance Luna Rosa
    Behold
        Red dream
Rose candy

Lipstick on my collar
    Instant replay
Inseparable eyes

Boxing gloves
Proper landing
Victory ahead

Convincing
Belly laugh!

Tears of the sun
　　Splash hit
Eye of the river

Holiday hopes
　　Don't overlook
Heaven's creation

Flood level
    Pass due payment
Bountiful desert

Unlawful act
    Lucky switch
Optimistic outcome

Ideal shadow
      Persistent threat
Boxing gloves

Wise
      Under pressure
Idiot

Spirit of desire
    I'll have another –
Lasting love

Verbal assault
Who left who
    Good at goodbye

Inner demons
It's a journey
Sick love

Corporate chapel
City hall

Virgin girl
    Stop who's that?

                                     Church social
                                     Full of joy
                                       Prayer boy

What a catch!
    Virgin girl

Love conquers virgin girl
He's the one!

There they go
Trading kisses
True romance

I love you honey
Imitation
I cried a tear

Mean bone
    Divulge
Easy attitude

Stone Sober -
Pleasant surprise
Love you more!

KINDRED HOPES

Our dream
      Lost in the fog
Touching rainbows

      Rose-colored boxing gloves
      Catch that dream

Promises to keep
You like that
Pure bliss

Virgin girl
Wedding prayer
He's the one!

Defining hope
    I came to praise
Broken promise

Cracked glass
    Decision reversed
The brick

Uphill battle
    No more misery
Headed for heaven

Burning shore
    Somewhere on the beach
Add water

I came to praise
The day you have made
Hope and change
Wise

Penny coin toss
Up with the birds
Sunset catch

Daring bride
Last kiss
Virgin girl

Blackout
Next success
Light the night!

On my toes
Blind ambition

Just make believe
World of trouble
Still beautiful

Stone heart
Break away
Unbroken spirit

Unbroken spirit
Return
Validity

Quality interest
Only you

Spirit grabber
    Break away
Stone heart

      World of trouble
      Get rid of
      All this commotion

Instant war
    Valid objection
Dreams of peace

Boxing gloves
Scrapple
Victory ahead

Secret pleasure
Always thinking
New heaven

Faith prevails
Hope and change
No more misery

Keep on dreaming
    Ready to fight
Another secret

Penny coin toss
    Up with the birds
Headed for heaven

Favorable outcome
    I cried a tear
Full of joy

Sober on Sunday
    Promises to keep
Just before pure bliss

Prayer boy.
Virgin girl.
    Cheers to you
        Keep on dreaming!

True romance
    Forever for always
'Til the end

Do you mind heaven's creation?
Holiday hopes?

Pure bliss
Launch away
Easy song

Analyze the odds
First of spring

Sea smoke
Launch away
Shiny finish

Fleeting Hope
I do not know
You are true

No more misery
No fear
No more talk

Joseph A Pasquale

Icy dawn
Change of seasons
Fields of gold

I call hopes and wishes
Holy plan

Anytime baby
Mine again

Appendix
(Horse Racing Names)

Act of madness
Add water
All this commotion
Always a suspect
Always thinking
Analyze
Analyze the odds
Another chance
Another secret
Anytime baby
Art of confusion
Baby touch
Backscatter
Behold
Belly laugh
Better way
Between
Blackout
Blame angel
Blind ambition

Bored stiff
Born in a breeze
Bountiful desert
Boxing gloves
Break away
Bridge builder
Bridge jumper
Broken promise
Buoy
Burning shore
Catch that dream
Cat 'n Bird
Change of seasons
Cheers to you
Cheese on
Chosen facts
Christmas carol
Chocolate ice cream
Church Social
City hall
Clean mind
Conscience
Contemplate
Convincing
Corporate chapel
Cracked glass
Dance Luna Rosa
Daring bride
Decision reversed
Defining hope
Divulge
Do you mind

Don't overlook
Dreams of peace
Easy attitude
Easy river
Easy song
Eden ridge
Entrusted
Expect kitten
Eye of the river
Eye of the wind
Faith prevails
Famous fact
Fashionably late
Favorable outcome
Fields of gold
Final tale
Fire on fire
First of its kind
First of spring
First punch
Fleeting Hope
Flood level
Fool me once
Forest dew
Forest mouse
Forest waltz grace
Forever for always
Full of joy
Get rid of
Gift of a star
Girl crazy
Golden bubbles

Good at goodbye
Good intent
Graceful image
Grass runner
He's the one
Headed for heaven
Heaven's creation
Hide the evil
Holiday hopes
Holy plan
Hope and change
Hopes and wishes
Hoppity
I call
I came to praise
I cried a tear
Ideal shadow
Icy dawn
Ideal shadow
Idiot
I do not know
I'll have another
I love you honey
Imitation
Infinite wisdom
Inner demons
Inseparable eyes
Instant replay
Instant war
It's a journey
I've got issues
I've seen the future

Jumping on clouds
Just before pure bliss
Just in speight of it
Justify
Just make believe
Keep on dreaming
King dollar
Kisses for love
Lakeside sunset
Lakeside surprise
Last kiss
Lasting Love
Laughing matters
Launch away
Lay it on
Let me sleep on it
Life happens
Light the night
Lipstick on my collar
Look at that
Looking for a smile
Look the other way
Lost for words
Lost in the fog
Love conquers
Love you more
Lucky switch
Making sure
Master of excuses
Mean bone
Midnight rumble
Mind reader

Mine again
Moon over Montana
Moral high ground
Morning breeze
Mountain on fire
Mouse trap
Mr. Bully frog
Mystical stones
Next success
New heaven
Nobody else
No excuses
No fear
No more misery
No more talk
Not for truth
Nothing but a smile
Off duty
Of note
Only you
On my toes
On the cusp
Optimistic outcome
Orbit
Our dream
Owl's run
Pacific wind
Pass due payment
Passing reminder
Path dependent
Penny coin toss
Pepper and salt

Persistent threat
Pleasant surprise
Prayer boy
Pop of color
Potential danger
Prayer boy
Promises to keep
Proper landing
Pure bliss
Pure perfection
Quality interest
Raining lemons
Ready to fight
Red dream
Red hot salsa
Retrospection
Return
Riding alone
River otter
Rose candy
Rose-colored
Sad Story
Scrapple
Sea foam
Sea smoke
Secret pleasure
Shiny finish
Sick love
Skip the talk
Snowy pleasure
Sober on Sunday
Somewhere on the beach

Space shuttle
Spirit grabber
Spirit of desire
Spiritual warfare
Splash hit
Still beautiful
Stone heart
Stone sober
Stop who's that
Storm the hill
Stormy river
Stun
Sunset catch
Surprise cameo
Tampered character
Tears of the sun
The brick
The day you have made
The ghost b dancing
The last cup
There's no doubt
There they go
Tiki bar logic
'Til the end
Touching rainbows
Trading kisses
Tricky escape
Troublesome waters
True concern
True romance
True wisdom
Trout

Unbroken spirit
Under pressure
Understanding
Under the rain
Unlawful act
Uphill battle
Up with the birds
Validity
Valid objection
Valid pursuit
Venomous state
Verbal assault
Victory ahead
Violet blue
Virgin girl
Visual effect
Watch your words
Web cam
Wedding prayer
What a catch
What gives
Who left who
Will make way wise
Winning element
Wise
World of trouble
You are true
You like that
You're wonderful
Yummy bear
Zero out
Zimbabwe

About the Author

Joseph A Pasquale is an American author who writes in a variety of literary genres including poetry, memoir, theater, film and fiction. He is a prolific writer who has penned over 65 books.

In 2019, Pasquale was published in the Hollywood hardback, "Literary (and other) Celebrity Doodles" Volume II.

He was also spotlighted in the Hollywood hardback, "The Musso & Frank Grill" (Published 2019). He is a regular writer-in-residence at Musso & Frank Grill in Hollywood, California.

Pasquale loves animals and has just completed an animal-inspired poetry series (12 books) titled *Journey of the Horses* and another collection *Dear Sparrow*. Within the first book series, he penned special *International* book editions for readers worldwide. Included in this series are books penned for Ireland and England.

Pasquale actively reads his poems in San Francisco, LA, and NYC. He is planning a reading tour to England, Ireland and Europe in late-2021.

www.ingramcontent.com/pod-product-compliance
Lightning Source LLC
Chambersburg PA
CBHW020328090426
42735CB00009B/1452